Bright-Eyed
Athena

in the stories of Ancient Greece

Richard Woff

BRITISH MUSEUM ██████ PRESS

Richard Woff was a teacher and then a lecturer in education at the University of London. He is now Deputy Head of Education at the British Museum where he organizes the Museum's provision for young visitors. He practises his storytelling on his daughters.

For Kate and Amy

© Richard Woff 1999

Richard Woff has asserted his right to be identified as the author of this work

Published in 1999 by British Museum Press
A division of The British Museum Company
46 Bloomsbury Street, London WC1B 3QQ

A catalogue record for this book is available from the British Library

ISBN 0 7141 2103 7

Designed by Carla Turchini
Printed in Slovenia by DELO tiskarna d.d. by arrangement with Korotan Ljubljana d.o.o.

Front cover: Detail of Athena from a red-figure *krater* (mixing bowl)
by the Berlin Painter, Department of Greek and Roman Antiquities, British Museum.

Contents

About Athena and Athens

To the ancient Greeks, Athena was one of the most important goddesses. She was the daughter of Zeus, the king of the gods, and a fierce, warlike goddess. She protected great male heroes such as Herakles, Odysseus and Perseus and was always in the front line of battle on behalf of her father. Athena combined her warlike nature with inventive intelligence. She was the first to tame horses and she invented the chariot and more peaceful skills like playing the pipes and spinning and weaving. She was particularly important to the people of Athens. Although Athens is now the capital of Greece, in ancient times it was one of a number of independent Greek cities.

One of the most famous landmarks in the world is the Acropolis at Athens, a rocky hill at the centre of the city. On top of the Acropolis are the remains of the Parthenon, a huge marble temple of Athena. The outside of the Parthenon was richly decorated with sculptures of gods, heroes, people and animals. Inside the temple was a 12 metre (40 ft) tall statue of Athena made of gold and ivory. Over the years, the great statue was taken away and lost in a fire and the Parthenon itself was converted first into a church and later into a mosque. After being badly damaged in an explosion in 1687, the temple began to deteriorate. In the early 1800s, Lord Elgin, the British ambassador to Turkey, removed most of the remaining sculptures and brought them to London, where they still are, in the British Museum.

In ancient Athens, the beginning of the new year came in midsummer and was the time for the celebration of Athena's birthday. The Athenians held a festival called the Panathenaia, which means 'all-Athens'. Every year they walked in a procession up the Acropolis, bringing a new robe or 'peplos' for the ancient wooden statue of the goddess. This statue lived not in the Parthenon, but in a smaller temple nearby. They also made sacrifices to the goddess. Every four years the Athenians celebrated the Panathenaic Festival on an especially splendid scale, with athletic and other competitions. The prizes for the winners of the competitions were large jars of the finest Athenian olive oil.

All the stories in this book link together with each other, and with the complicated, fascinating character of Athena, with her worship, her temples, her city and her people.

Gods, Monsters, People and Things

You will understand most of the characters, places and things through the stories themselves, but here are some that need a bit more explanation.

Lydia	An ancient country in what is now Turkey. Lydia was famed for its wealth.
peplos	A piece of clothing worn by Greek women. It consisted of a large rectangle of fine woollen cloth, which was folded around the body and fastened at the shoulders with pins. Athena is wearing a peplos in the picture on page 8.
aegis	A short, fringed cloak made of goat skin, which Zeus and Athena wear around their shoulders and chest. It has magical powers of protection. Athena is wearing the aegis on page 4.
Olympos	The highest mountain in Greece. Olympos is the home of Zeus and the other major gods and goddesses.
Titans	Ancient powers of nature, the children of Sky and Earth. Prometheus and Epimetheus are children of the first Titans.
Pandora	The first woman. Her name means 'all gifts'. You will understand why when you read the story and find out how she was made.
gorgons	Three monsters with snakes for hair, whose look turned people to stone. Only one of the gorgons, Medusa, could be killed.
Okeanos	One of the original Titans. The ancient Greeks believed that his river flowed around the furthest edges of the world.
nymphs	Young female powers of nature who inhabit trees, streams, lakes, hills and the sea.
Eleusis	A town about 14 miles from Athens, which was the most important centre for worship of the goddesses Demeter and Persephone. Only people who had been initiated into or taught about the 'mysteries' of the goddesses could take part in the worship.

Spinning the Thread

'The thing I remember about Stratyllis is the wool on her lips. When she could not wind any more thread around the spindle, she bit through the thread with her teeth – she still had strong teeth – and fine wisps of wool stuck to her dry, cracked lips.

Sometimes we all worked in silence, concentrating on our different tasks. The only noises were from the spindles if they struck the ground or the baskets as someone pulled out another bundle of raw wool or from the loom as the shuttle moved across or as my mother lifted the threads forwards and then back in a steady rhythm.

At other times we talked or sang, but most of all we told stories. At least, the others told stories. When I was your age, I just listened. I had heard most of the stories already, but each was new in the way it was told. Every woman had her own style of telling, her own way of weaving the story so that you became entangled in it until the moment came when you stopped doing whatever you were doing and hung there, still, caught, waiting for the end.

Stratyllis was the best storyteller. I can still see those little scraps of wool moving on her dried-up lips as she told the story of Arachne.

Arachne lived in the rich land of Lydia. Her father was a dyer who sold his yarns to wealthy houses, even to the king himself. Their colours were those of the glittering dark sea, of the gleaming leaves of the laurel, of the gushing blood of a goat, of the hilltops touched by the last rays of the sun. But Arachne was the jewel of the household; she wove the yarns with perfect skill, making clothes that clung to and flowed around the body. And she was proud of her art. One day she even hinted that the goddess Athena could not match her weaving. It was the tiniest hint, but it was enough.

Athena took the form of an old woman and went to visit Arachne. She found her in the courtyard of her house with the other women. It was still early and she had not yet started to weave. Two looms stood ready, the threads were set, and the yarns lay in baskets arranged around them. Arachne welcomed the old woman and offered her a chair and some water to drink.

'I have heard of your skill,' said the old woman 'but I do not think that youthful freshness is ever a match for the experience of age. Let me see what you can do.'

On this wine jug you can see a woman spinning. In her left hand, she holds a wooden rod called a distaff with a bunch of wool attached to it. With her right hand, she draws out some strands of wool, which she has attached to a spindle with a weight on it. The woman spins the spindle so that it twists the strands into a thread. She is finely dressed, has carefully styled hair and wears a twisted bracelet on each wrist.

The jug was found in a grave. Making cloth was one of the most important activities for a Greek woman. If the grave was a woman's, the picture shows one of the ways she was expected to spend her life.

'If you simply want to criticize my work,' Arachne replied, 'I will not co-operate with you. If you are challenging me, I accept, for then you must prove yourself too. We will weave two cloths at the same time, here, today, and in the evening we will see whose skill is the greatest.'

So the two women began to weave. The skimming of their shuttles and the lifting of the threads created a regular pattern of sound and movement that was only broken when they paused to float in a different coloured yarn or to make a knot or pull out a loop of thread. A crowd of women slowly gathered. At first they came just from the house of Arachne, but then from neighbouring houses and streets as word spread of the contest.

As the morning wore on, the pictures they were weaving into their cloths began to emerge. The old woman had chosen the battle between the gods and the giants.

The battle of gods and giants appeared on the peplos which was presented to Athena's ancient statue and also in the sculptures on the east end of the Parthenon. To the Greeks, the battle was a symbol of the victory of civilization over nature and probably also of their victory over the Persians in the wars of the fifth century BC. This sculpture is part of an altar from Pergamon in Turkey. Athena drags a giant by his hair while her snake bites at his chest. You can see the shape of her helmet, her shield and her aegis with the head of Medusa in the centre. Notice the giant's agonized expression and the different textures the sculptor has carved: the muscles of the giant's body, the feathers, the snake's scales, the folds of Athena's peplos.

ONCE, WHEN THE WORLD was still young, the earth gave birth to a race of giants. The bodies of the giants ended in writhing snake-tails. They possessed tireless strength and wildness in their hearts.

They recognized no limits to their desires and craved power over the whole world. They resented the rule of Zeus and the other gods and growled and grumbled their anger. Gradually their resentment grew until it exploded in a scream of frustration and the giants began their attack. They uprooted huge pine trees for clubs and snatched up enormous rocks as if they were pebbles on a seashore. Then, in order to reach the gods in their sky-palace Olympos, they lifted whole mountains and piled them one on top of another and started to climb.

Zeus called together the other gods and the devastating battle began. Zeus himself led the attack, hurling lightning bolts into the seething mass of giants, and the air was filled with smoke and burning and the stink of sulphur. Poseidon, Zeus's brother, rose from the sea. Driving his trident deep into the earth, he levered up an immense chunk of land and crushed a giant beneath it. Hephaistos pelted the giants with lumps of red-hot iron. Hermes, wearing the helmet of death, moved invisible among the enemy, killing them before they knew they had been hit. Ares revelled in the slaughter of war. The arrows of Apollo and his sister Artemis rained down from above, while Herakles used his bow to pick off the giants one by one.

In the midst of them all strode Athena, daughter of Zeus. Her chest was covered by the protective aegis skin. In her left hand she gripped her shield and in the right her spear. The crest of her helmet nodded as she struck at the giants. She darted quickly towards the giant Enkelados, but he saw her coming and fled. Athena looked around her and put down her shield and spear. She lifted up the island of Sicily, tearing it from its roots, and hurled it at him.

The Giants, and also the Titans, were the children of Ge, the Earth. The Giants stand for chaos and wildness. By defeating them, Zeus brings order to the universe. This bronze statuette shows a Giant about to hurl a rock during the battle with the gods. His face shows the effort he is putting into the throw and his muscular body shows his great strength.

That mass of rock and earth and fields and mountains caught him in mid-step and buried him beneath its bulk. Even now you can hear the snorts and moans of Enkelados from deep below Sicily's volcanoes. Athena let out a cry of victory that filled the giants' hearts with terror.

The crowd of women in the courtyard muttered with fearfulness as they watched the old woman working. The power and majesty of the gods was clear.

Arachne worked just as quickly, with her dark eyes fixed on the threads as she sent the shuttle across and back, across and back. She was not weaving pictures of death and violence, but of desire.

First she wove a dark, gaping chasm and from it rose Hades, brother of Zeus and god of the dead. The four black horses that drew his gold chariot reared in the unaccustomed light of day as Hades snatched up the lovely Persephone to be his queen. Then she wove the bed of Hephaistos. On it lay his wife, Aphrodite, wrapped in the arms of warlike Ares. But cunning Hephaistos had set a net above the bed and trapped them in it as they embraced. Then he invited the other gods to come and see the lovers' disgrace and the laughter of the gods was heard even on earth. Next Arachne wove a dense forest. Through the forest raced Apollo, who was filled with desire for Daphne. She ran from him in desperation, out of the shade of the trees and across the mountains. He dodged bushes and leapt over rocks in his pursuit. Just as he caught her, just as he set his hand on her, just as his fingers tightened their grip, she called out for rescue and the goddess of earth changed her into a laurel tree.

In threads of gold, silver and purple, Arachne wove all the secret loves of Zeus, the loves he hid from Hera, his queen. Here Zeus had changed himself into a swan and was nestling up to Leda. Here as a bull, he was carrying off the beautiful Europa. Here as a shower of gold, he caressed Danaë.

AT THE CENTRE OF THE CLOTH was a hillside and on it Zeus lay with the lovely Metis. Zeus's body was dark upon the gorgeous flowered bank, while the skin of Metis shone silver pale. When three months had gone by the goddess of earth brought Zeus dreadful news. Metis would give birth to a daughter, but her next child would bring destruction on Zeus and all the other gods. Zeus acted. He immediately went in search of Metis.

In the fine building with its tall white columns sits Zeus, king of the gods. This must be the palace of Mount Olympos. Next to him stands Aphrodite, goddess of love and attraction. Her son, the winged Eros, is at her side. In her right hand Aphrodite holds a magic wheel which was used to attract lovers. These three are plotting the latest of Zeus's love affairs because of what you can see below the building. This is happening on earth. A beautiful woman named Leda is planting a kiss on a swan. She draws the swan's head towards her with her hands and the swan stands on tiptoe to receive the kiss. The swan is Zeus in disguise. Later, Leda will lay two eggs!

There are several other figures shown on this pot. On the upper left is Astrape, goddess of lightning. On the upper right sits a woman who represents Eleusis, the town which was sacred to the goddesses Demeter and Persephone. The painter put the names of most of the figures next to them so that they could be recognized easily.

When he found her, he lifted her in his hands, opened his vast mouth and swallowed her whole.

Some months later, Zeus woke up with a headache. As the hours passed, the pain grew worse. Zeus lay in a darkened room at the centre of his palace with his head buried in soft cushions. Hera sat with him wiping his brow with snow-water and giving him honey-sweet nectar to drink. But nothing helped. As the agony increased beyond bearing, Zeus lost his temper. He stormed from his room and swept through the palace. He howled and raged, tearing at his throbbing brows, swinging his mighty head from side to side and smashing everything that came into his path. Down on earth, the animals looked up anxiously at the dark clouds gathering, and as they heard the rumbling in the sky they scuttered under rocks and into burrows.

Then Zeus bellowed, 'Hephaistos!!! Bring your axe!!!'

Hermes would have been there in an instant, but Hephaistos was much slower. His shortened, twisted leg made it hard for him to move fast. When he arrived, he found Zeus sitting on his throne. Zeus was quiet and his body seemed calm, but his bulging eyes showed the desperation and the torment inside.

'I can stand no more,' groaned Zeus. 'There is a movement, a fretting, struggling movement inside my head. The agony must be released. Use your axe.'

Hephaistos did not dare to disobey. He raised his axe above his head and with all his strength brought the blade down. Zeus's skull split open and from the gaping hole, in full armour, with a deafening war-cry, leapt Pallas Athena, the bright-eyed goddess, daughter of Zeus and Metis.

The light in the courtyard of Arachne's house was beginning to fade, but when the women saw the pictures Arachne wove, they smiled at the passions of the gods and at the tricks of lusty Zeus. And they thought of their own husbands and of their sons and they whispered and giggled and then laughed out loud.

The old woman was surprised to hear laughing. She put down her shuttle and stood back from her loom so that she could see what her young rival had done. Then the anger swelled inside her and she rose to her full height and cast aside her disguise and showed herself for who she really was. The women fled or fell to the ground, and their cries filled the house as Athena roared at Arachne.

'You show no respect. First you claim that you are a better weaver than I am and then you dare to show the scandals of my family, here in public for humans to snigger at!'

Furious, the goddess snatched up her shuttle and struck Arachne with it across the head. Again and again Athena struck. Arachne tried to ward off the blows with her arms. Then, as the raw red weals rose on her face and the hot tears poured down her cheeks, she turned and fled into the house. When she reached her room, she took a length of her father's finest purple yarn, and standing on a stool she fastened one end to a roof beam, looped the other around her neck, knotted it and kicked the stool away.

Bright-eyed Athena could see what the girl had done and did not wish to be in the presence of death. With a nod she made Arachne shrink. Smaller and smaller she grew and her skin turned hard and black. At the same time her belly swelled and her limbs were drawn inside her until just her eight fingers stuck out, four on each side. At last, Athena turned away and left Arachne hanging by a thread to spin and weave her webs forever.

Stratyllis's voice tailed off. The rest of us glanced at each other and smiled and shared the moment with a sigh. Then we went back to our spindles and our baskets and our looms.'

The Beginning of Evil

'Myrrhine – she was your great grandfather's sister – interrupted our thoughts. 'Arachne forgot that it was Athena who gave her the gift of weaving in the first place. If it had been up to the other gods, we would all still be as naked as when we were born. We hide in our clothes and reveal to each other only what we want to reveal. Clothes are like words; we can use them to get what we want.' Then she told us about Pandora.

In the earliest days of the reign of Zeus, when the world was still young, Prometheus, the Titan, made men. He took handfuls of clay and moulded them with his fingers, forming limbs and bodies and heads. Then Athena blew into their nostrils and gave them life. Their lungs filled with air, their flesh grew warm and their eyelids flickered open. Zeus despised these dismal creatures and was about to strike them with his lightning-bolts, when Prometheus came to him on their behalf. He promised Zeus that men would worship him and make the gift of sacrifice to him. He even offered Zeus first choice of the best parts of the victim. But Prometheus tricked the king of the gods. He sacrificed a bull and then cut it into pieces. He put the finest meat to one side, covering it with the animal's heart and lungs and liver. Then he took the white bones and wrapped them in succulent, yellow fat. When Zeus saw the foul innards of the bull, he was disgusted and chose what he thought were the rich, fatty thighs of the animal.

Prometheus was delighted – he had won for men the very best meat. But Zeus's fury swelled inside him and he took away from men the gift of fire. Now they could not cook their food and once the sun had set and the chill of night crept over the world, they had no source of warmth except to huddle together, shivering in the deepening darkness. Soon the men began to sicken and die. Prometheus was overwhelmed with pity for his defenceless children. He climbed up to the top of Mount Olympos, to the sky-palace of Zeus. There, he stole a sliver of fire and brought it back to men in the hollow stalk of a fennel plant.

This sculpture shows a heifer being led to sacrifice. It comes from the marble frieze that surrounded the inner building of the Parthenon. Most people think that the frieze shows a version of the procession at the Panathenaic festival. The young man on the left is alarmed at something happening behind him and pulls on the heifer's halter. The halter was made separately of bronze and then attached to the frieze. It is now lost.

Zeus could take no more of Prometheus's insolence. He wanted complete revenge on men, but sending death in a firestorm of lightning would be too easy and too quick. The punishment of men must be slow, inescapable and for all time.

He called for Athena and Hephaistos and explained his plan. Hephaistos took some of the clay from which Prometheus had made men and from it he moulded the first woman. Then all of the gods gave her a gift. Aphrodite gave her charm and a beauty that men would yearn to possess. Hermes made her quick-witted, clever and treacherous. The goddess Persuasion and the Graces gave her bracelets of twisted strands of gold. Next Athena covered her in the finest clothes, woven through with silver threads, which caressed the shape of her body. She hid the enticing face of the woman behind a veil and put around her head garlands of flowers still damp with dew from the meadows. Finally, amidst the flowers, Hephaistos set a diadem. It was made of gold and on it he had worked all the animals of the earth and the sea. Then Athena breathed life into her and named her Pandora.

Now Hermes brought Pandora to earth, to the house of Epimetheus, brother of Prometheus. Epimetheus was not as clever as his brother; he lived his life from day to day, not thinking of the future, not seeing where the twisting paths of time were leading. When he saw the living gift Hermes had brought to him, he could not see beyond her modest smile, beyond the glance of her eyes, beyond the radiant surface of Zeus's gift. He accepted Pandora as his wife.

One day, as Pandora stood at her loom weaving a cloak for Epimetheus, her concentration wandered from the steady rhythm of her work. Her attention was caught by a box, high up on a shelf, just below the ceiling of the room. She had not noticed it before; she had been too distracted by the newness of her life. She paused for a moment, shuttle in hand. She remembered something Epimetheus had said. One morning, soon after she had arrived in his home, Epimetheus had said to her,

'Prometheus once told me that it is better not to know everything; that some secrets are not to be revealed. In this house, what is open to you is open and what is closed is closed. Respect my wishes and do not seek to see what should not be seen.'

Deep in Pandora's mind tendrils of curiosity began to spread. She left her loom and dragged a stool over to where the box sat on the shelf. She climbed on to the stool, stood on her tiptoes and stretched up. The shelf was very high, but with the tips of her fingers she could just make contact with the underside of the box where it jutted out from the shelf. She slid the box out until she could take its weight on her hands. It was much heavier than she had expected – it was almost as if something inside it was moving. She brought the box down and sat with it on her lap. She tried the lid, but the box was shut tight. She turned it round and noticed two small catches, one on each side of the lid. She put her thumbs against them and began to push. Once more she heard Epimetheus's words, '… some secrets are not to be revealed.' She paused. She realized her mouth was dry, but she had gone too far now. '… what is closed is closed … should not be seen.' Her heart was pounding as she forced the catches aside and lifted the lid.

A chaotic vortex of brutality and hatred, a blizzard of disease and starvation, of suffering and violence erupted from the box and billowed across the world to devastate human life from that time onwards. Our happiness is fragile and the slender thread of our life is easily cut.

Myrrhine stopped the story there. She always did. We all knew why, but didn't have to say it. We also knew that there was a little more to the story, that when the evils of the world had all flown out, under the lid of the box lingered hope.'

The Deadly Glance

'You could never tell what would spark off a story. Sometimes it was something somebody said or some bit of news one of the women had picked up from a friend. Sometimes it was the time of year or a wedding or a funeral or one of the festivals. Sometimes the story just came from nowhere. We would all be lost in what we were doing, not talking or looking at each other and then a story would creep up on someone.

One day Kalonike stepped back from her loom. She had just finished a piece of cloth. It had a deep border of sphinxes, sirens and other winged monsters picked out in purple, and around the very edge she had worked some gold thread into the pattern. As she stood gazing at her work, the story of Perseus snaked its way into her mind.

This is the goddess Hebe wearing a dress which is decorated with patterns and rows of animals. The peplos woven for Athena's statue may have looked something like this. Very few examples of cloth survive from the ancient Greek world, but we know from literature and from images such as this one that cloth could be elaborately woven and coloured. The textiles that the women of the household produced were symbols of their hard work and of the family's wealth.

King Akrisios was a happy man. He ruled the abundant land of Argos and the people of his kingdom lived in peace. His wife had died some years ago, but he had a daughter named Danaë. Her beauty and laughter filled his life with joy. She was growing up quickly and Akrisios looked forward to finding her a fine husband. He longed for the carefree embrace of grandchildren. A simple message from the gods shattered the king's hopes. On one of his visits to the temple of Apollo, the holy priestess whispered to him his terrible future: he would meet his death at the hands of his daughter's child, his own grandson.

Akrisios was desperate to avoid the death the priestess had foretold. He could not bring himself to kill Danaë, so he decided to hide her away, out of the sight of men. In spite of her tears and her pleading, he locked Danaë in a room deep underground, cut into the rock, lined with bronze, where the light of the sun never penetrated. Just one old woman was allowed to take the princess her meals. But nobody can build a barrier against Zeus. The great god had seen Danaë's loveliness. He changed himself into a shower of liquid gold and seeped into her prison to be with her. When Danaë's baby boy was born, she named him Perseus.

It is hard to hide the cries of a baby and Akrisios soon discovered Perseus. Although he realized that his life was beginning to unravel, he still could not bring himself to destroy his only family. So he ordered one of his carpenters to build a wooden box. He put Danaë and Perseus inside and nailed on the lid. Then Akrisios took the box to the shore and set it adrift, handing over his daughter and her child to the sea. He stood and watched as the box floated to the horizon, where it was engulfed by the swell. Then he turned in sadness back to his palace.

The sun's chariot had crossed the skies many times when, on the coast of the far distant island of Seriphos, a fisherman hauled up a battered and salt-crusted box in his net. His heart leaped at the thought of gold and silver, but when he forced open the lid and discovered a young woman and her baby, he realized he had found an even greater treasure. He had no family, no prospect of children to care for him in his old age. The fisherman recognized from her clothes and from the glow of her loveliness that Danaë was of royal blood and could never be his wife, but he took her and Perseus into his home. The little family lived together contentedly. The fisherman cared for and respected Danaë; she learned to spin and weave and tended a small field nearby. Perseus looked after the goats and fished and mended nets. He grew into an energetic young man, strong and good looking, but he knew little of the intricate web of life.

Polydektes was the king of Seriphos. He learned of the presence of a strange woman on his island. Enticed by stories of her loveliness, he decided he had to see her for himself. As his birthday approached, Polydektes ordered all those who lived on Seriphos to come to his palace and bring him a gift. As soon as he saw Danaë, he knew he had to possess her. But her son was a problem; he would be sure to try to protect his mother. The king had to get rid of him. When it was the fisherman's turn to present his family's gift, he opened his sack and unrolled a small rush

Greek artists always showed gorgons full-face. They gaze out at you with their wide eyes, the mouth fixed in a vicious grin, the tongue sticking out. This gorgon is part of a handle of a large bowl for mixing wine. She does not have snaky hair, but lifts her skirt to reveal that she has snakes for legs. You can also find gorgon faces on shields and other pieces of armour and around the edges of the roofs of buildings. The monster's gaze keeps off evil and protects the warrior, the building or, as here, the wine. Athena wore a gorgon's head in the middle of her aegis.

mat at the feet of the king. Then on the mat he laid out two mullet, caught that very morning, their scales still gleaming silver. Next to them he placed a crumbly white cheese.

Polydektes howled with laughter. 'Is that the very best that you can scrape together from your wretched little life? Is that what you think is suitable for your king? You insult me with your smelly fish and stinking cheese.'

Perseus's anger flared up at once and before his mother could stop him, he cried, 'If these are not good enough for you, name the gift you want. Go ahead. I will bring you anything you want.'

Polydektes smiled. He sat back in his throne. 'Far from here, in the west, where the sun god dips his chariot into the encircling river of Okeanos and brings darkness to the earth, there is a desert. The three gorgons live there. Their hair writhes with snakes, their tusks are sharper than a boar's, their wings are quicker than an eagle's. A single glimpse of a gorgon's face drains the warmth, softness and moisture of life from humans and turns them to stone. Medusa is the only gorgon of the three who can be killed. You told me to name my gift_.' The king leaned forward, stared into the eyes of Perseus, and spoke low and calm, 'Bring me the head of Medusa.'

High on Olympos, Athena heard the king's words. Deep inside the goddess there still glowed an ember of resentment at Medusa for an old insult. She called to Hermes to accompany her and the two children of Zeus set off for Seriphos. They found Perseus that evening sitting at the foot of an oak tree wrapped in his cloak. He had started immediately on his search for the gorgons and was tired from a long day's walking in the heat of the sun. Athena spoke to him softly.

'Perseus, the law of my father Zeus prevents me from doing your task for you, but I can help you on your way. The Nymphs can give you three gifts which you need to win Medusa's head, but you have to find them first. Only the three ancient Graiai, the Grey Sisters, know where the Nymphs live and they will not tell you unless you force them to. Hermes will guide you to their home. Watch the sisters, watch them carefully before you do anything.'

Perseus set off again with Hermes as his guide. Soon he was walking in a land of grey. The earth was a fine ash in which his feet left perfect tracks. A thick layer of smoky clouds filled the sky. Rocks lay scattered around. Their surfaces were veined with cracks and crumbled to powder at a touch. As they reached the mouth of a narrow gorge, Hermes stopped. 'You will find the Grey Sisters here,' he said. 'Go silently and watch them.'

There was a sudden flutter of wings. Hermes disappeared and a sparrow darted away into the clouds.

Perseus crept forward slowly. He crouched low behind a large rock and very gradually peered around it. A little way ahead of him sat three old women. They were bundled up in thickly woven cloaks the colour of cracked pepper. Their waxy skin was deeply lined and their dank hair was plastered in thick hanks over their shoulders. They were muttering and mumbling, and from time to time one would stretch out a bony arm and take something from one of the others. Perseus waited and watched.

Finally, he saw what they were doing. Instead of two eyes each, the three Graiai had just one eye between them. Instead of each sister having her own teeth, they had just one tooth between them. When one of the sisters wanted to gnaw a few crumbs from the crusts of stale bread that lay around them, she asked for the tooth and pushed it into her gums. When one of the sisters had to keep watch for trespassers, she took the eye and slipped it into one of her gaping sockets. Perseus waited and watched again. At last he saw where their weakness lay. When one of the Graiai eased the eye out of her socket and reached out to pass it to one of her sisters, for that moment, none of them could see and the eye was there for the taking. Perseus waited. Soon it was time for a change of watcher. The sister with the eye eased it from her face and held it out. Perseus darted from his hiding place and snatched the eye from the tips of her fingers.

At first each sister thought that one of the others had dropped the eye and scrabbled blindly around in the dust complaining about their carelessness. Then their frustration rose and they screamed in anger and fear. Perseus sat and watched them for a little while, enjoying his victory. Then he spoke.

'Listen to me, you hags. I am Perseus and I have what you are looking for. Tell me where I can find the Nymphs and you will have your eye back. If you refuse,' he let the eyeball nestle in the palm of his hand, 'I will squash the jelly out of it!' The three old women let out a howl of rage and scuttled towards the sound of Perseus's voice, but he skipped away from them with ease. 'This is your last chance. Where are the Nymphs?' The sisters knew they could do nothing and told him what he wanted to know. 'Thank you, ladies. Now here is your sight back,' and he tossed the eye towards the women. It rolled along the ground gathering dust and grit on its sticky surface. Then he turned away and left them to their search. After he had gone some way, a cry of triumph – or was it pain? – told him they had found it.

Perseus passed out of the land of the Graiai and entered a thickly wooded valley. Here he found the Nymphs, who welcomed him graciously and gave him the three gifts Athena had mentioned. First, he pulled on a pair of winged boots, which gave him the power of flight. Second, he set on his head the helmet of death, which made him invisible and brought him under the protection of Hades. Third, he put across his shoulder a magic bag to contain Medusa's head. Finally, Hermes came to him again and gave him a hooked sword. Its keen edge was jagged like the blade of a saw. Then Hermes pointed out the way and Perseus sped off towards the land of the gorgons.

Soon he came to a desolate place. No plant grew there. Bare rock stretched away to the horizon. No river, no stream, no trickle of water slaked the thirst of the arid earth. The gods avoided this barren waste. Only the all-seeing eye of the sun gazed down on its emptiness. High above this desert, Perseus soared in the vast vault of the sky, searching for the gorgons. He found them dozing, nestled together in a sandy hollow. Athena had sent the sleep god to drip drowsiness into their eyes. Perseus hovered overhead. He was unsure which of them was the mortal Medusa, but Athena, unseen, guided his hand. Turning his face away, he stretched out his left hand and grasped Medusa's hair.

This wine cup shows an unusual version of the story of Perseus. We have many pictures of Perseus running away from the gorgons, but here he is chasing them. You can just see Perseus on the left with his sword and winged boots. The gorgon, who is probably Medusa, is wearing the skin of an animal with its paws knotted around her shoulders. The other two gorgons are ahead of her, running around the other side of the pot.

At once, a squirming mass of snakes entwined his arm. He felt his throat tighten at their disgusting touch. He raised his sword and struck. There was a gasp, almost a sob and then a long, sinking hiss. Perseus thrust the writhing head into his bag and sped away. Behind him, Medusa's headless body thrashed about and her sisters awoke. They could not see Perseus, but quickly they caught his scent and with a screech of grief and fury gave chase. They hunted Perseus across the desert and over the waters of Okeanos, but his winged boots and the guiding hand of Hermes swept him away from them.

At last, Perseus arrived back in lands where humans lived. Far below him, at the end of a rocky finger of land jutting out into the sea, he could see something moving. As he swooped down, he saw that a young woman had been chained to a rock and that a crowd of people was gathered on the nearby beach watching. At that very moment, the crowd roared out in fear and pointed out to sea. Perseus slowed down to see what was happening. Deep below the sparkling surface of the water a vast, dark shape appeared. It rose swiftly and burst from the sea in a sputtering surge of salt spray. Perseus reached into his bag, gripped Medusa's head and dived down from the sky.

The people on the beach had barely glimpsed the sea monster's enormous scaly head and its gaping jaws bearing down on their princess Andromeda, when time seemed to pause for a moment and then jerk again into motion. Suddenly, instead of a monster there was a new, misshapen rock out at sea. A young stranger was standing before their king holding Princess Andromeda's hand. Then the whole crowd cheered and wept with joy. The king embraced his daughter and announced a royal wedding and a month of rejoicing.

It was over a year later that Perseus and his wife arrived back in Seriphos. When he reached his old home, he found his mother gone and the fisherman alone. The fisherman explained that Danaë had resisted the king's desires in the hope that Perseus might return. Now she thought that her only hope was with the gods and had taken refuge at the altar of Zeus. King Polydektes and his men had surrounded her there and were starving her into submission. Perseus left Andromeda with the fisherman and taking his bag set off to find his mother.

When Polydektes saw Perseus, he mocked him. 'So you are back at last. It has taken you a long time to bring my gift, but I am always happy to have a birthday present, even a late one. I suppose you have Medusa's head in that little bag. I can't say that I think much of the wrapping!' The king and his followers roared with laughter, but when Perseus drew the

This wine jug shows the killing of Medusa. On the left is Perseus, who plunges his sword into Medusa's throat. You can also see the other gifts he needed to kill her: the bag across his shoulder, the hat of invisibility and the winged boots. Notice how he looks away from Medusa as he kills her. He is almost the double of Hermes, who looks on from the right. Hermes is able to look at the gorgon, for as a god he is protected against her gaze.

Herbert Cole probably made this drawing early this century as an illustration for a book of Greek myths. On the left you can see the sea monster amidst the waves. Andromeda is standing on the right near a rock. Perseus is wearing his helmet and winged boots and carries his sword. In some versions of the story of Medusa, Perseus uses a highly polished shield as a mirror. This means that he can see to cut off Medusa's head without looking directly at her. Cole has given Perseus his shield and has set the gorgon's head in the middle of it.

gorgon's head from his bag, their limbs hardened, their blood turned to sand in their veins and the laughter stopped. Then Athena came to Perseus and gently took the head from him. She was wearing her aegis skin across her chest. In its very centre she set the gorgon's face to paralyse her enemies with terror and she fringed the skin with the snakes.

Perseus made the faithful fisherman king of Seriphos – he learned to be a wise king and his people grew to love him. Then, with Andromeda and Danaë, Perseus set off back to his birthplace, back to Argos to see his grandfather. When they reached Argos, Akrisios was gone. He had heard of his grandson's imminent return and had run away to escape the death the priestess had foretold. Perseus was hailed as the new king.

Some years later, in a distant land, Perseus was competing in an athletics competition. When it was his turn to throw the discus, he threw so far that the discus hit an old man in the crowd and killed him on the spot. Nobody knew the old man, so Perseus had the body brought back to Argos for burial. No-one recognized the old man until Danaë came to mourn. She stood over the body and gazed down at the lifeless face of her father Akrisios.

This kind of carving, where a layer of stone of one colour is cut away to uncover a layer of a different colour is called a cameo. This cameo is set in a gold ring. It shows how stories can change over time. It is from the Roman period, many centuries after the story of Perseus was first created. Perseus still has his winged boots, his sword and shield, but here he is able to look at Medusa's head after he has cut it off. Also, Medusa's face is no longer that of a hideous monster, but of a beautiful, though sad, young woman. It is now the attractive power of her beauty that turns men to stone if they see her.

Pigs and Pomegranates

'I was very small when Stratyllis told me about the pigs. Every year, in the spring, the women of the city climb the hill opposite the Acropolis. They carry with them piglets, just a month or two old, and special pastry cakes. When the women reach the top of the hill, they throw the pigs and the cakes down a deep pit. In the autumn, around the time of sowing, the women come back. Three of them climb down the pit, gather together what is left of the pigs and bring the remains back to the surface in baskets. Then they mix the seed corn into the baskets and give it to the men to sow on the land. When you are older, you will see all this for yourself.

We also take pigs along the Sacred Way to Eleusis. The Sacred Way joins us, the children of Athena at the heart of Athena's city, to the Great Mother, Demeter, in her temple at the very edge of our territory. We take the pigs as gifts for the Great Mother, but also for her daughter, Persephone. Stratyllis told me about them too.

Once, when the world was still young and the reign of Zeus was still new, Persephone was picking flowers on a hillside in Sicily. It was eternal spring in those days and the slopes of the mountains were thick with violets, hyacinths, crocuses and narcissus. Persephone was alone. She had wandered away from her friends in search of the best flowers for a garland for her mother Demeter. It was restful up there; she could hear the distant voices of her friends far down the hillside. Somewhere off to her left was the grunting of a herd of pigs and, even further away, the occasional whistle from their swineherd. As she stretched out her hand to pluck one last delicate yellow narcissus, the earth at her feet gaped open and from the chasm rose Hades, brother of Zeus and god of the dead. The four black horses that drew his golden chariot reared in the unaccustomed light of day and snorted steam as their icy breath met the warm air of the upper world. Zeus had promised Hades a bride and he had come to claim her. The chariot plunged back into the blackness and the earth closed up once more. The lovely young goddess was gone.

Persephone's friends looked for her until nightfall, but all they could find was a scattering of broken flowers. They ran in terror to bring the news to her mother Demeter, the news that nobody ever wants to bring, the news that a child is lost. They left the hillside empty except for a puzzled swineherd who wandered searching for his pigs, which seemed to have disappeared completely, without trace, as if the earth had just swallowed them up.

When she learned that her child was gone, Demeter felt a hollow, aching bewilderment deep within her. With a howl of anguish she sped to Sicily. There she crossed and re-crossed the mountainside, over and over and over and over again, unwilling to admit that there was nothing there, positive that if she looked just that one more time, Persephone would be there, that she would hear her sweet one's voice, hold her warm body, kiss her cherished face. It could not be that she was not there, she simply had not looked enough. She could not leave, not without one final, scrabbling, desperate hunt. She lit two torches from the fires of Mount Etna and by their light she scoured every field, every gully, every cave, every wood, every fold and crease of the mountainside until, in the first, watery light of morning, she sat down and cried.

Eventually, when she had wept herself out, Demeter arose, wrapped a dark cloak around her shoulders, re-lit her torches and broadened her search. As she wandered, she ignored her care of the earth and of the

All ancient Greek temples had sacred areas around them called sanctuaries. This pig comes from the sanctuary of Demeter at Knidos on the coast of Turkey. Worshippers of Demeter and Persephone often sacrificed pigs or gave statues or models of pigs as gifts. This one was dedicated to Persephone by a woman named Plathainis.

The swineherd who lost his pigs when Hades carried off Persephone was called Eubouleos. It is said that he became the first priest of Demeter and Persephone at their sanctuary at Eleusis near Athens.

things that grow. The grass in the pastures turned yellow and brittle, the flowers shrivelled, leaves began to curl, the figs rotted and the skin of apples still on the trees grew wrinkled and brown.

After nine days, Hekate, the goddess who bears the moon in her hands, came to meet Demeter and spoke to her. 'Demeter, giver of wonderful gifts, I heard Persephone's cries, but I do not know what god or mortal has snatched her away, for I saw nothing. However, of all the gods only Helios sees everything – you must ask him.'

And so the two goddesses came to the great sun-god and asked him what he knew. Helios reined in the horses of his chariot and paused as he crossed the sky. 'Demeter,' he replied, 'I respect you and I pity you for the loss of your child. You will know the truth, for I see everything. The one who is guilty of taking your daughter is none other than Zeus himself. He has given her to his brother Hades as his bride. Hades has taken her away beneath the earth. But come, goddess, put an end to your grief. Persephone will be the great queen of the underworld and will receive constant respect and honour from humans.' Then he called to his horses and they sped off into the sky like swift-winged birds.

When she heard Helios's words, Demeter's sorrow turned to fury and she abandoned the company of the gods for the cities and fields of humans. Yet still she neglected her duties and the land became weak and barren. Trees now drove their roots deeper into the earth in a futile search for nourishment. Tender shoots turned black and rotted before they reached the surface of the earth and, even in the finest soil, seeds failed to swell and lay, infertile, lacking the force that would give them life. The spectre of hunger haunted the world and people and animals grew thin.

One day the four daughters of King Keleos of Eleusis left the city. They were beautiful girls, with the flower of youth upon them. They carried bronze jugs to bring water back from the spring to the house of their father. Near the spring, they came across a woman sitting in the dust at the side of the road. When they saw her they stopped and greeted her. The woman just sat there with her ragged clothes trailing in the dirt, her head veiled, her eyes unfocused, gazing into the distance. The eldest of the girls squatted alongside and taking the woman's hand asked, 'Who are you and where do you come from? What has brought you down so low as to sit here away from other people in a wild place at the edge of the town?'

The woman turned her head to see the girl whose kind words betrayed her goodness. 'My child,' she said, 'my name is Doso and I come from Crete. A band of pirates tore me from my home and carried me off to sell as a slave. They brought their ship ashore just down the coast from here,

This statue from Knidos shows Demeter sitting calmly on a throne with a soft cushion. She probably held an offerings bowl or a torch, which reminded people of her night-time search for Persephone. Originally, there may have been a statue of Persephone herself standing alongside. Demeter and her daughter were so closely linked that people often used to speak of them simply as 'The Two Goddesses'.

Demeter has her head veiled. In ancient Greece, brides usually veiled their heads and sometimes so did older married women. The veil was a sign of modesty. Not all ancient Greek goddesses were shown like this. Not far from Demeter's statue, there was a very famous statue of Aphrodite, the goddess of love, which showed her naked, just getting out of the bath.

Bright-Eyed Athena   31

but while they feasted and drank, I slipped away into the darkness. Now here I am, alone, far from home, hungry and racked with grief. Sweet girls, may the gods grant you fine husbands and strong children if you will just take pity on me and take me to your parents' house. I am a willing worker and can do all the tasks that women do. I will weave cloth, watch over the house and care for children.'

The girl glanced at her sisters and smiled, 'Humans must endure what the gods grant even if they do not want to, for the gods are stronger than us. But do not fear, you have found safety now,' she said. 'Queen Metaneira, our mother, is looking for a nurse for our baby brother. Our parents have wanted a son for many years now. He has been a long time arriving and so is a welcome and much cherished child. If you help to bring him up, you will earn eternal thanks from our family and support in your old age.' With these words, the princess raised the woman to her feet and led her to Eleusis.

When the girls explained what Doso had told them, their parents were at first unsure. However, the stranger had an air of calm, a trace of hidden power, and they welcomed her into their palace. Metaneira offered her wine, but she would only drink a mixture of barleymeal, water and fragrant pennyroyal. She would not sit on the fine chair they offered her, but preferred a low stool. There was a sadness about her. But when Iambe, one of the maids, joked with her and then fell off a stool and ended up with her skirts over her head and her legs in the air, then for the first time, Doso laughed. The king and queen handed the care of their baby son to her.

Doso was devoted to the baby. She cared for him at all times. For hours on end she would sit in the shade of the palace courtyard. He snuggled into the crook of her arm as she rocked gently back and forth and sang him songs and told him stories. When the sun had dipped in the sky, she would climb up to the roof of the palace and look out across the barren countryside with its withered grass and stunted trees and she would let the warm breeze blow her hair and swirl across the baby's face. Even at night Doso would not leave the child, but brought his cradle into the hall of the palace where she slept wrapped in her cloak by the fireside.

The king and queen and their daughters soon began to notice changes in their new-born baby boy. He seemed to become stronger every day. His skin was a glowing, peachy pink, his arms and legs were chubby, his eyes were bright and he looked out for his loved ones and chuckled when they spoke to him. In a land full of starvation, a land where no plants would grow, one little baby thrived and offered hope to all.

One night Queen Metaneira awoke with a start. She could not tell if it was a noise or a movement, but something had broken through her sleep and caused her to shiver with misgiving. She could not fall asleep again, so she rose from her bed and made her way towards the hall of the palace. She felt drawn there, thinking that perhaps the warmth of the fire and the murmuring of her child would bring her rest.

The door into the hall was open and she could see the light from the fire flickering inside. When she reached the doorway she stopped suddenly, unsure of what she could see, unable to make out exactly what was happening within and sensing deep inside her that perhaps she should not know. She could see Doso silhouetted against the light of the fire with her back to her. She was holding something in her arms and rocking to and fro. She was singing softly. The queen glanced towards the baby's cradle – it was empty, the sheets trailing over the side. She moved further into the hall so that she could see more clearly.

Doso was leaning right over the great hearth. Stretched along her left arm, she held the naked body of the baby deep in the fire. With her right hand cupped she lifted the flames and let them fall in streams over his head and arms and legs and soft belly, just as a mother bathes her child in warm water and lets tiny rivulets trickle along the folds of the baby's skin. The little boy looked up at her and smiled and gurgled and waved his arms and legs in joy as he revelled in the touch of the flames. Metaneira caught her breath.

Doso turned, and seeing the queen, snatched the baby from the flames and clutched him to her. She seemed suddenly to grow, becoming straight and tall. Her face and whole body radiated an awesome power and the queen knew she was in the presence of a goddess.

Demeter, the Great Mother, sister of Zeus cried out, 'You mortals are so foolish and so ignorant. My fire burns away mortal weakness leaving power and strength that cannot be quenched. Your son would have become deathless, a god, a replacement for my dear lost daughter. Now that cannot be.' She paused. 'Yet, for your goodness to me, I will offer you gifts. Build me a temple, carry out sacrifices for me, pour blood-red wine and milk into the dust of the earth. Do these things in my honour and I will teach you and your people secret rites and I will reveal to you objects and speak to you words that hold out hope even when death comes to claim you.' She laid down the baby and was gone.

Immediately, the king called together the people of Eleusis and told them what the goddess Demeter had ordered. They worked day and night to build her a temple and the goddess came and sat inside, shunning the company of gods and humans.

Now great Zeus was deeply worried. He could see the earth was dying and that all the inhabitants of the earth would perish too and that the gods would no longer receive the gifts of sacrifice from humans. So he sent Iris to Demeter to ask her to relent in her anger and return to the company of the gods, but Demeter would not change her mind. Then he sent all the gods and goddesses to take gifts to Demeter, to surround her and to beg her to bring life back to the world. Still Demeter sat in her temple and refused to give way until she had her daughter back with her and could see her dear face and hold her in her arms. Zeus had no alternative. He sent for Hermes and ordered him to go to Hades and command him to release Persephone.

In an instant, Hermes was on his way. He slipped unseen over the decaying cities, past smoking funeral pyres, over arid, famine-stricken fields, far, far to the west until he passed through the gates of the underworld and reached the shadowy, echoing halls of the king of the dead. He came to a stop before the throne of Hades. Persephone sat apart from Hades, her back turned to him, her heart filled with longing for the light and warmth of the world above.

'Forgive me, uncle,' Hermes began, 'but your brother Zeus has sent me to order you to return Persephone to her mother. The world above is dry and barren and all living things are near to death. The gods can no longer rely on the worship and sacrifices of humans. Your sister Demeter will not relent and make the earth fertile again until she has her daughter back and sees her dear face and holds her in her arms. I am here to escort her.

The Temple of Artemis at Ephesos in Turkey was one of the Seven Wonders of the World. Here you can see a carving from one of its huge columns. Hermes is on the right. He carries a rod with a twisted end. This shows that he is a messenger and should be allowed to pass easily to his destination. You can also see the shape of a broad-brimmed hat, which he has pushed to the back of his neck. Hats like this are very important if you are travelling in the sun. One of Hermes's jobs was to guide the souls of the dead down to the Underworld. That is what he may be doing here; the woman standing in front of him may be dead or about to die and he is waiting for her.

This is one side of a tomb found in southern Turkey. The sculpture is in a Greek style. At the sides, winged harpies carry off small figures of the dead. Their embrace seems protective in spite of their clawed feet. In the middle, a large man sits on a throne. He may be a dead ancestor of the family. A woman is bringing a bird as an offering to him. He is holding two pomegranates. The ancient Greeks connected pomegranates with growth and fertility because of the numerous seeds they contain.

Do not resist, or once the souls of those still left on earth have descended to your gloomy kingdom, there will be no more of them and the numbers of your subjects will never increase again.'

Hades recognized the force of necessity and nodded agreement to Zeus's command. He called for his golden chariot to be harnessed and made ready for the journey. Now Persephone's heart leapt with joy at the thought of once more feeling her mother's arms around her and she raised her eyes and turned towards Hades and Hermes. Then the king of the dead took a pomegranate from a table at his side and cut it in two. He offered half to the lovely Persephone. Hades knew what he was doing – the taking of food would be a pledge to return to the underworld, a sign that she belonged there. Persephone had neither eaten nor drunk since entering the realms of the dead. Yet even in the cold darkness beneath the

earth, a young girl can feel hungry. She saw the seeds glistening ruby red
in their creamy beds. She took the fruit and raised it to her lips. Her teeth
bit into the pomegranate's brittle, blushing skin and she sucked out the
veins of sweetness. Hades smiled. Then the chariot was brought and he,
Hermes and Persephone rode to the palace of Zeus.

As soon as Demeter heard the news, she rushed to Olympos to catch
her beloved daughter in her arms, to kiss away her tears, to feel again the
soft warmth of her child's embrace. Even when Zeus told her of the
pomegranate and ordered that Persephone would always have to spend
one third of every year as Hades' queen, Demeter could find no more rage
in her, no more grief, just a sense that some part of her child had slipped
away from her. Together, mother and daughter returned to Eleusis and as
they went, they brought fruitfulness back to the land.

The Panathenaic procession followed a road known as the Sacred Way from the edge of Athens to the Acropolis. The other end of the Sacred Way was at Eleusis, where Demeter and Persephone were worshipped. On this drinking cup, Demeter stands on the left holding a torch and some stalks of corn. Persephone, on the right, has handed her stalks to a young man seated on a throne with wheels and wings. He holds an offering bowl. This is Triptolemos. Demeter and Persephone taught him how to grow corn and he travelled the world teaching other humans. This painting is from a pot which was found in a tomb. The ancient Greeks connected together death and fertility and this connection was probably at the heart of the mysteries of Demeter and Persephone.

The seeds began to sprout, buds unfolded, apples and figs and grapes swelled. They taught humans how to plough and sow and harvest and how to unlock the riches of the earth, so that during the winter, when Persephone was in the realm of Hades, they would have enough to eat and could prepare for her return in the spring. Finally, just as Demeter promised, they revealed their mysteries to the people of Eleusis, the secret of how to loosen death's grip.

From the very first time that Stratyllis told me their story, I longed for the moment when I would learn the mysteries of the Great Mother and her daughter, Persephone. Now I have been to Eleusis and I have seen what is revealed and heard what is spoken.'

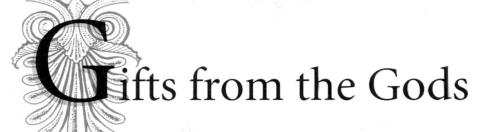

Gifts from the Gods

'You never knew your great-grandmother. I remember once she came in to my room late in the evening. She had been out that day watching the procession to Athena's ancient statue. My father was getting ready to go out with some friends. They were waiting for him in the courtyard of the house. I could hear the sound of their conversation and laughter. My mother was flushed with excitement and eager to talk, but there was nobody to listen except me. It was a treat to have her to myself and I nestled in her arms as she told me about all the people and the horses and chariots and the goddess's new dress. Something she had seen on the temples must have stuck in her mind, because that was when she told me about our city's earliest times.

The first people who lived here were born from the earth itself. They made their homes at the foot of the Acropolis, the high place, the great rock that rises above us. From here they could look out across their fields to the shimmering surface of the sea. Their first king was Kekrops and he built his palace on the top of the Acropolis. The soil in these parts was fertile. The sea gave up a rich harvest of fish. The hills around gave fine stone to build with. The people were prosperous and happy, but the town had no name.

Kekrops was a clever man. He knew that if the town was named after one of the gods, it would always have divine protection. One day he made a sacrifice to Zeus and the gods of Olympos. At the centre of the Acropolis was a large heap of ashes, charred wood and bones, the remnants of many other offerings to the gods. Here, Kekrops's men lit a fire and got ready grains of corn, water and the sacrificial knife. Then a fine white bull was led up the slopes of the hill from the fields below. Kekrops washed his hands and sprinkled water on the bull. It tossed its head, nodding its agreement to become a gift to the gods. Then the king scattered the grain and cut the bull's throat with a single slashing blow. His attendants quickly skinned the animal and cut it into pieces. Then they wrapped its thigh bones in rich fat and put them on the fire.

Kekrops raised his hands to the sky and prayed. 'Mighty Zeus, king of the deathless gods, lord of the thunder and the lightning bolt. If ever you

This pencil drawing shows how the hill of the Acropolis rises up above the city of Athens. It was clearly a good place to defend and the earliest rulers had their palace up there. The Acropolis also became the most important religious place in Athens. You can see several of the temples on top. The Parthenon is on the right. In the centre is the gateway to the summit of the hill. The drawing was done by the British architect C. R. Cockerell in the early 1800s. Cockerell went on to design several buildings in a Greek style back in Britain.

have been pleased with the rich smoke of our sacrifices to you, hear me now. Our town is wealthy, our people are blessed with all the gifts the earth brings forth and our children grow up vibrant and strong. Which of the gods wishes to grant us their name and to receive special honours from us forever?'

Zeus heard Kekrops' words and called upon his favourite child, Athena, to go and receive the gifts of the people. But Poseidon, Zeus's brother, disputed his decision. He argued with the king of the gods, claiming that the new town was close to the sea and that those who drew upon the riches of the sea must pay their chief respects to him. Zeus could not settle the argument and sent Hermes to speak with Kekrops.

Hermes scorched a path to the palace of the king. He found Kekrops and explained Zeus's dilemma. Kekrops immediately saw his opportunity. 'Hermes, swift-footed son of Zeus, you bring me sad news. If no solution to this argument can be found, my town will be left with no name and no guardian. Would Zeus allow mere mortals to decide? Perhaps if Athena and Poseidon were each to offer us a gift, we could choose which of them would receive our special honours and respect?'

When Hermes brought Kekrops's answer to Zeus, the king of the gods was delighted. He did not like the idea of choosing between Athena and Poseidon. The prospect of facing the resentment of either of them filled him with dread. He nodded his head and granted Kekrops's request.

From the earliest glimmerings of dawn, the people began to gather on the Acropolis. They picked their way up the rocky slopes, following the narrow goat tracks between boulders and thorn bushes. They found Kekrops and his whole household already waiting at the edge of a large open space at the east end of the great hill. In the centre of the space stood the bright-eyed daughter of Zeus and her uncle, Poseidon, the earth-shaker. When the whole population had assembled, Kekrops gave the signal for the contest to begin.

It was Poseidon's turn first. 'Mortals!' he bellowed. 'Your future depends on the protection of the gods and apart from Zeus himself, I am the most powerful of those who live on Olympos. I will demonstrate to you the strength I possess. Choose me and I vow that I shall never unleash this power against you, but I will use it to crush your enemies.' With these words, Poseidon raised his fearsome trident, stretching every muscle and sinew of his broad shoulders, and then, with a roar, he plunged it into the earth. As the triple points penetrated deep into the living rock the whole of the Acropolis quaked and groaned. The people huddled together in terror and babies began to cry. Then, surging out of the rock came a foaming torrent of salt water which gushed into a hollow forming a deep, dark pool.

Athena stepped up. She took her spear and without a word drove it into the ground. Then she stepped back. As the people looked on, the straight shaft of the spear began to buckle and twist. Branches and twigs sprouted from it. Buds swelled and opened into slender, dark green leaves. As the breeze caught the leaves, they flickered over to show their silver undersides. Soon small grey-green fruits appeared and fattened in their thousands. It was as if the whole life of the tree had been compressed into moments. Then Athena stretched out her hand and plucked some of the fruits from a branch. She stepped towards the people. Raising her hand in the air she tightened her grip. As she did so, she crushed the fruits and a thick, clear, green liquid began to ooze between her fingers. She dripped this oil on to the hands of Kekrops and his people. They were amazed as it coated their skin with a satin softness. A fragrance enticed them to taste the oil, cautiously at first with the tips of tongues and then rolling its pungent sweetness around their mouths. 'Citizens,' said Athena, 'this is the olive tree. Use it in whatever way you wish. It will delight your senses and enrich your lives. Its gifts will make you the envy of the world. Let it be the eternal symbol of my care for you. Let this be my city. Name it Athens.'

This silver coin from Athens shows the head of Athena. You can see her helmet clearly. The other side of the coin shows an owl, which was Athena's bird. The slang for these coins in the ancient world was 'owls'. You can also see a sprig of olive leaves and olives. The silver for the coins came from rich mines at Laurion to the south of Athens. The slaves who dug out the silver suffered dreadful hardship. As many as 30,000 of them may have been working the mines at the height of production. One wealthy Athenian made a large amount of money by hiring out 1,000 of his slaves for work in the mines.

Athena's Children

'Athena has never abandoned her city. After the Persians invaded and destroyed her temple and burned her sacred olive tree, Athena returned and the blackened stump of the tree put forth a fresh green shoot. She seems to be everywhere. No matter where you are outside the house, there are those moments when you glance up. There, rising above you on the summit of the Acropolis are Athena's temples, at the very heart of the city. You are a little older than I was when I was chosen to serve the bright-eyed goddess. I was just eight. That is very young to spend a whole year away from your family. You are a better age. My mother and the other women were so proud of me. They kissed and hugged me. I even saw tears in Theano's eyes. She had also served the goddess and knew that the time was right. It was Theano who told the story of Pandrosos.

Under the protection of Athena, the young city of Athens prospered. King Kekrops ruled with justice and wisdom. He had three daughters named Herse, Aglauros and Pandrosos. These three girls were clever and skilful. Athena herself had taught them how to set up the threads on a loom and weave intricate fabrics of fine wool. Each year, on the goddess's birthday, they had repaid her by weaving a new robe for her ancient wooden statue. However, Athena was worried. Kekrops was getting old and had no son to take over the kingdom from him.

One night, Herse, Aglauros and Pandrosos lay asleep in the king's palace on the Acropolis. The god of sleep had dripped drowsiness in their eyes and had freed their minds from the care of the day. Athena came to them as they slept and whispered to them, calling them down from the palace to a place by the river, where the women of Athens went to wash clothes. The three girls awoke and quickly sneaked out of the palace and down the rocky slopes of the Acropolis. The moon was bright and made it easy to follow the path to the washing-place.

There Athena was waiting for them. So as not to dazzle the girls with her radiance, she had taken the form of one of the women of the palace, an attendant of their mother. The bright-eyed goddess spoke to them softly and the three girls knew her voice. 'You are like daughters to me. Your gifts and the care with which you tend my temple show me that I

So many owls nested on the slopes of the Acropolis that ancient Athenians often used to complain about being kept awake by their hooting. The ancient Greek word for an owl was connected with the word for bright or gleaming, probably because of the owl's large, alert eyes. Some people think that owls were closely associated with Athena because she was originally an owl-goddess.

When the Persians invaded Greece, the Athenians decided to fight by sea rather than on land. So they abandoned Athens, which was then destroyed by the Persians. Just before the sea battle, as the leader of the Athenians was making a speech, an owl flew up and landed at the top of the mast of his ship. The Athenians and their Greek allies went on to smash the Persian fleet and win a magnificent victory.

can trust you. Your father is old and you have no brother to whom he can pass on his power. Yet the city must have a king, and not a foreigner, but one from the very land of Athens. Do as I ask you now and you will bring Athens not just a king but everlasting good fortune.' Then she picked up a round wicker basket and handed it to Herse. The girls saw immediately that the lid of the basket was tied shut. 'Follow my instructions and do not disobey me. Take this basket back to the Acropolis and place it inside my temple. Be careful as you go. Its contents are beyond value. No matter what happens, do not show it to anybody else and do not open it. Remember my words.' An owl screeched and scudded across the river into the olive groves and the goddess was gone.

The three girls took their orders seriously. They went slowly back towards the Acropolis. They took it in turns to carry the basket. It was surprisingly heavy and they did not want to drop it because of tired arms.

Their journey back took a long time. Dawn was already streaking the sky with pink when they reached the top of the hill. Suddenly Aglauros, who was carrying the basket at the time, let out a shriek. 'Something moved inside,' she cried. Herse took the basket from her sister and held it a moment. She too could feel a shift of weight, an undulating, swaying motion. 'I must see,' she stammered and began to fumble at the fastenings on the lid. Aglauros joined her. They put the basket on the ground and loosened the ties.

Pandrosos was horrified. 'Think of Athena's words,' she cried. 'Leave it closed, leave it closed.' She pleaded with her sisters, the tears streaming down her cheeks, but Aglauros and Herse could not hear her. They were drawn helplessly to what was inside the basket. Finally, they scrabbled the last fastening loose and lifted the lid.

Inside the basket seethed the coils of a tongue-flickering human snake child. Then Athena's howling fury, the incandescent brilliance of her presence, shattered the two girls' bodies and shredded their

This vase painting probably shows Kekrops. His staff is the sign of a king and he has a bowl from which to pour wine as an offering to the gods. Kekrops's body ends in a snake. The early kings of Athens were associated with snakes. The ancient Greeks thought of snakes as being creatures of the earth – they live in the ground and are always in contact with it. The snaky kings may be linked with the idea that they were born from the earth itself and did not come to Athens from somewhere else.

45

These two women are sitting on a comfortable-looking couch. The one on the left has a footstool. She wears a headband and a large ring on her finger and may have been holding a mirror or a fan. They both wear coloured clothes and the woman on the right has bright red shoes. Some people think they are Demeter and Persephone. In ancient Athenian society women had very clear roles to play in the home and in religious ceremonies. Poorer women, foreign women and slaves were seen outside the house more often than wealthier, freeborn women, who had little independence. Whoever these women are, they lean together in intimate conversation. They remind us that talk and close relationships between women can flourish even in an oppressive world.

minds. Herse and Aglauros hurled themselves from the Acropolis on to the jagged rocks below.

Pandrosos closed the lid and, trembling, picked up the basket. Carefully she carried it to Athena's temple and placed it inside. Then she ordered a special space to be marked out nearby and a high wall to be built around. There Pandrosos stayed, cut off from her family and friends, tending the precious gift of Athena. Her only contact with the outside world was with two young girls who joined her each year to help her in her duties. They took in the supplies of grain and honey and woollen thread that the people left for them on top of the rocky Acropolis.

One day old Kekrops died and a new king of Athens appeared. His name was Erichthonios. His first act was to order a festival to celebrate the birthday of Athena. He called together the people in a great procession up to her temple on the Acropolis. They carried with them a birthday gift made by Pandrosos and her companions – a fine new robe woven in purple and gold with the battle of the gods and the giants – in which they dressed Athena's ancient wooden statue. They led up cattle and sheep for sacrifice and the smoke of their offerings rose to Olympos. Then Erichthonios decreed that this festival should take place every year and that it should be for all the people of Athens. The Athenians obeyed the orders of their new king even though nobody knew where Erichthonios had come from. He had simply emerged from the shadows inside Athena's temple. Some said he was the son of Pandrosos. Some said he was born from the earth itself. Some said he was Athena's child, but that couldn't be. Pandrosos kept the secret.

Theano finished. The women hugged me and congratulated me again, then went back to work at their looms. While they worked, they talked about their own youth. As I listened, I sensed that their lives were woven together, that each of them lived the experience of the others. They had all carried baskets in Athena's great procession, even though only Myrrhine actually walked on the goddess's birthday. They had all ground the grain for the sacred snake's honey cakes, even though only Stratyllis got her hands floury. Now I was about to become a thread in that web of women. We would all have prepared the loom to weave Athena's new peplos, even though I would be the one to knot the threads. No-one needed to explain what it means to serve the bright-eyed goddess. When you hear the story of Pandrosos, you know.'

Further Reading

British Museum Activity Book: The Ancient Greeks, British Museum Press, 1986.
British Museum Colouring Book: Ancient Greece, British Museum Press, 1997.
Fergus Fleming, *Greek Gazette*, Usborne, 1997.
Leon Garfield and Edward Blishen, *The God beneath the Sea*, Kestrel Books, 1970.
Fiona MacDonald, *Inside Story: A Greek Temple*, Simon and Schuster, 1992.
Fiona MacDonald, *How would you survive as an ancient Greek?*, Watts, 1995.
A. Millard, *Pocket Guide: Ancient Greece*, Usborne, 1992.
Anne Pearson, *Eyewitness Guide to Ancient Greece*, Dorling Kindersley, 1992.

Illustrations

The objects pictured are in the British Museum Department of Greek and Roman Antiquities unless otherwise stated

Cover and p. 4: Detail of Athena from red-figure *krater* (mixing bowl) by the Berlin Painter: Vase E468.

pp. 1 and 42	Athenian silver tetradrachm, BM Coins and Medals Dept.
p. 7	White-ground *oinochoe* (wine jug) by the Brygos Painter: Vase D13.
p. 8	Battle of the gods and giants on Great Altar of Pergamon: Bildarchiv Preussischer Kulturbesitz, Berlin.
p. 9	Bronze statuette of giant hurling a rock: J. Paul Getty Museum, Los Angeles, 92.AB.9.
p. 11	Apulian *loutrophoros* (water carrier): J. Paul Getty Museum, Los Angeles, 86.AE.680.
p. 13	Black-figure *kylix* (wine cup): Vase B424.
p. 15	Section from south frieze of the Parthenon: Slab XLIV.
pp. 16-17	Gold diadem from Melos: GR 1856.12-13.1 (Jewellery 1607).
p. 18	Black-figure *dinos* (mixing bowl) by Sophilos: GR 1971.11-1.1.
p. 20	Bronze *krater*-handle from southern Italy: GR 1873.8-20.99 (Bronze 583).
p. 23	Attic *kyathos* (drinking cup) with Gorgon: J. Paul Getty Museum, Los Angeles, 86.AE.146.
p. 25	Black-figure *olpe* (wine jug) by the Amasis Painter: Vase B471.
p. 26	Herbert Cole, drawing of Perseus rescuing Andromeda: BM Dept of Prints and Drawings, 1932-7-15-41.
p. 27	Cameo gem of Perseus with Gorgon's head: J. Paul Getty Museum, Los Angeles, 87.AN.24.
p. 29	Marble pig from sanctuary of Demeter at Knidos: Sculpture 1305.
pp. 31 and 33	Statue of Demeter from Knidos: Sculpture 1300.
p. 35	Carved column base from the Temple of Artemis at Ephesos: Sculpture 1206.
pp. 36-37	South side of the Harpy Tomb: Sculpture B287.
p. 38	Red-figure *skyphos* (wine cup) by Makron: Vase E140.
p. 40	C. R. Cockerell, pencil drawing of the Acropolis.
p. 44	Detail of owl of Athena from Attic *kalpis* (water pot): J. Paul Getty Museum, Los Angeles, 86.AE.229.
p. 45	Red-figure *rhyton* (drinking vessel) by the Sotades Painter: Vase E788.
p. 46	Hellenistic terracotta group: Terracotta C529.